THE OLDWAYS
4-WEEK
MEDITERRANEAN DIET
MENU PLAN

MAKE EVERY DAY
MEDITERRANEAN

We want to thank the members of the
Mediterranean Foods Alliance for their generous
support in helping us promote the remarkable
health benefits of the Mediterranean Diet.

For information about special discounts for bulk purchases,
or about co-branding options, please contact
Oldways, 1-617-421-5500 or store@oldwayspt.org.

ISBN 978-0-9858939-0-3

The Oldways 4-Week Mediterranean Diet Menu Plan

For anyone who loves food, the flavors of tradition are too delicious, too meaningful, and ultimately, too important to give up. No organization understands this better than Oldways Preservation Trust. It was Oldways that, in conjunction with some of the world's top nutritionists and scientists, came up with the innovative Mediterranean Diet Pyramid.

— Cooking Light

Oldways, a nonprofit food and nutrition organization with a mission to guide people to good health through heritage, created the original Mediterranean Diet Pyramid in 1993. Since then, we have worked tirelessly to spread the word about this healthy and delicious way of eating.

This book is dedicated to the late K. Dun Gifford, founder of Oldways, who partnered with scientists, food and wine producers, policymakers, and chefs around the globe to document and celebrate the joys and benefits of the Mediterranean Diet.

You can learn more about Oldways at www.oldwayspt.org.

CONTENTS

INTRODUCTION

OLDWAYS 4-WEEK MENU PLAN

BONUS PAGES

MEDITERRANEAN DIET PYRAMID

A Contemporary Approach to Delicious, Healthy Eating

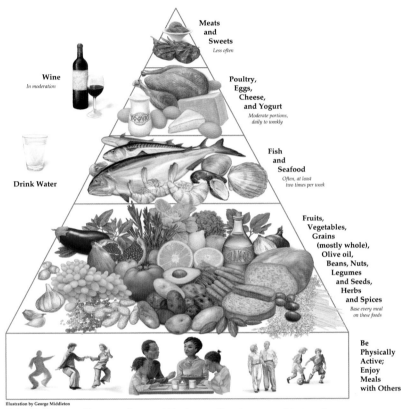

Illustration by George Middleton

© 2009 Oldways Preservation and Exchange Trust • www.oldwayspt.org

The Mediterranean Diet Pyramid is your guide to good food from the bottom (most important!) on up. Since the rest of this book focuses on food, we'd like to draw attention to the lifestyle activities that make up the base of the pyramid.

- Look for ways to be more active. Good food alone isn't enough to live a healthy life.

- Cooking and enjoying the pleasures of the table with family and friends contribute hugely to good health.

2

INTRODUCTION

Welcome to the
Mediterranean Diet

The Mediterranean Diet is not a diet, as in "go on a diet," even though it's a great way to lose weight and improve your health. Rather, it's a lifestyle, based upon the traditional foods (and drinks) of the countries that surround the Mediterranean Sea. Scores of leading scientists have rated this way of eating as one of the healthiest diets in the world—while millions of people like you have rated it one of the most delicious!

The Mediterranean Diet is all about cooking and eating simple, whole-some, minimally-processed foods, being active, enjoying delicious meals with friends and family, and (if you choose) drinking wine in moderation with those meals.

Best of all, you don't need to travel any further than your local supermar-ket to find all the ingredients you need. It's so easy and affordable to bring the remarkable Mediterranean style of eating to your own kitchen.

Once you make a few simple but profound changes in the way you eat to-day, you'll see how rewarding it is to follow this traditional eating pattern for the rest of your life.

All of these meals—and more—are part of the Mediterranean Diet, a way of eating with so many options that you'll happily eat this way from now on.

8 SIMPLE STEPS

Mediterranean Diet Food Rules for Good Health

While the Mediterranean Diet includes foods from Southern Europe, the Middle East, and North Africa, you don't need to travel any further than your local supermarket to discover its delicious flavors and fresh foods.

It's easy to bring the remarkable health benefits and affordable Mediterranean style of eating to your kitchen cupboards, your refrigerator, your counter tops, your stovetop, your oven, and your table every day. Embracing the Med Diet is all about making some simple but profound changes in the way you eat today, tomorrow, and for the rest of your life.

THE MENUS YOU'LL FIND ON THE FOLLOWING PAGES ARE BUILT UPON THESE 8 SIMPLE STEPS:

1. EAT LOTS OF VEGETABLES.

There are so many choices! From a simple plate of sliced fresh tomatoes drizzled with olive oil and topped with crumbled feta cheese to stunning salads, garlicky greens, fragrant soups and stews, healthy pizzas, or oven-roasted medleys, vegetables are vitally important to the fresh tastes and delicious flavors of the Mediterranean Diet. Can you fill half your plate with them at lunch and dinner?

2. CHANGE THE WAY YOU THINK ABOUT MEAT.

If you eat meat, have smaller amounts. For example, add small strips of sirloin to a vegetable sauté, or garnish a dish of pasta with diced prosciutto. As a main course, have smaller portions (3 ounces or less) of chicken or lean meat.

4

3. INCLUDE SOME DAIRY PRODUCTS.

Eat Greek or plain yogurt and smaller amounts of a variety of cheeses.

4. EAT SEAFOOD TWICE A WEEK.

Fish such as tuna, herring, salmon, and sardines are rich in heart-healthy omega-3 fatty acids, and shellfish including mussels, oysters, and clams have similar benefits for brain and heart health.

5. COOK A VEGETARIAN MEAL ONE NIGHT A WEEK.

Build these meals around beans, whole grains, and vegetables, and heighten the flavor with fragrant herbs and spices. When one night feels comfortable, try two nights per week.

6. USE GOOD FATS.

Include sources of healthy fats in daily meals, especially extra-virgin olive oil, nuts, peanuts, sunflower seeds, olives, and avocados.

7. SWITCH TO WHOLE GRAINS.

Whole grains are naturally rich in many important nutrients; their fuller, nuttier taste and extra fiber keep you satisfied for hours. Cook traditional Mediterranean grains like bulgur, barley, farro and brown, black or red rice, and favor products made with whole grain flour.

8. FOR DESSERT, EAT FRESH FRUIT.

Choose from a wide range of delicious fruits—from fresh figs and oranges to pomegranates, grapes and apples. Instead of daily ice cream or cookies, save sweets for a special treat or celebration.

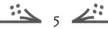

GET READY, GET SET, COOK

The best way to eat healthy, affordable food is to prepare it or assemble it yourself from good ingredients. If you're already comfortable cooking, that's great. If you're not in the habit of cooking, these two pages will tell you the essentials you need to know to make the simple dishes in our Mediterranean Diet plan.

Cooking Basics

- Exact measurements aren't usually important, unless you're baking. If our recipes say "1 can (14.5 ounces) of tomatoes," don't worry if your can is a little bigger or a little smaller.

- There are three main ways to cook food in your kitchen: in a lot of liquid or a little oil on the stovetop, or roasting/grilling/baking in the oven.

  To cook food in water (or broth), turn the burner on high until the water bubbles rapidly (boils), then turn it down until the water barely bubbles (simmers), and cook according to directions.

  To cook food in oil, heat a small amount of oil in a pan. Never let it smoke; that means it's too hot. Stir the food around in the oil frequently (sauté). Cook according to directions.

  To cook food in the oven, see recipe directions.

Equipment You'll Need

You don't need a lot of fancy gadgets to cook the meals in this book. You'll be fine if you have the following:

- a large skillet (fry pan)
- a few sauce pans with covers
- a large stock pot or soup kettle
- a measuring cup
- measuring spoons
- a sharp knife
- a vegetable peeler
- a grater
- a cutting board
- a can opener

- a few mixing bowls
- a colander or strainer
- a large mixing spoon
- dishtowel(s)
- pot holder(s)
- a blender or immersion blender

Stocking Your Pantry

Cooking is easier when you have basic ingredients on hand in your kitchen cabinets, refrigerator or freezer. Most of the basics on this list keep indefinitely, so you buy everything once, then just replace as needed:

Seasonings
- salt
- pepper
- oregano
- cinnamon
- cumin
- curry powder
- garlic cloves
- ginger
- sugar
- honey
- vinegar

Oils
- extra virgin olive oil
- butter

In the Freezer
- frozen shrimp
- frozen berries
- frozen veggies

Cans, Jars & Boxes
- black beans
- white beans (e.g. cannellini, navy)
- chickpeas
- dried lentils
- broth
- oatmeal
- bulgur
- brown rice
- pasta
- diced tomatoes
- tuna
- nuts and peanuts
- seeds (sunflower, pumpkin, etc.)
- dried fruit

Keep A List On The Refrigerator

When anything runs low, jot it down on the list. About once a week, buy replacements, perishable foods, and special ingredients for specific recipes, such as:

- fresh fruits
- fresh vegetables
- chicken, fish or meat
- bread and rolls
- eggs
- cheese
- yogurt

SUBSTITUTE INGREDIENTS

We've included a range of typically Mediterranean ingredients in our menus so that you can explore some new tastes. But we realize some of these ingredients may not be available in your store, or may cost more than other choices.

Here are some substitutes we recommend:

Original Ingredient	Perfectly Good Substitute
Romaine lettuce or Mâche	Baby spinach, any leaf lettuce
Brie or Goat cheese	Any spreadable soft cheese
Cannellini beans	Black beans, chick peas, lentils
Coconut milk	Almond milk
Croutons	Any cooked whole grain
Fennel bulb	Celery
Feta cheese	Parmesan cheese
Farfalle, Penne, Rotini, Ziti, Shells	Any shaped pasta
Herbs, fresh	Dried herbs (1/3 of original amount)
Linguini	Any long thin pasta
Olives, Greek, Kalamata, or black	Any olives
Onion, yellow, red, or Vidalia	Whatever onions you have
Pomegranate seeds	Dried cranberries
Swiss cheese	Any mild white cheese
Winter squash	Sweet potato
Whole wheat orzo	Any cooked whole grain
Zucchini	Any other summer squash

Although our recipes may be subtly different with these substitutes, they'll still be delicious.

 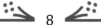

How to Use These Menus

The menus you'll find on the following pages are designed to take you on a 28-day journey through many of the delicious and satisfying tastes of the Mediterranean Diet. Unlike most diets, the Mediterranean Diet doesn't cut out all the good stuff and leave you feeling deprived. Because it features a wide variety of foods that are just naturally healthier and lower in calories, you'll find you can enjoy "good taste" and "good for you" at the same time.

A few pointers will help you get the most from our menus:

• Feel free to mix and match, taking a breakfast from one day, lunch from another, and dinner or dessert from a third day. You may find one breakfast you especially like and eat it day after day, or pick seven dinners you want to cook week after week. Follow your taste buds – this is not a rigid plan!

• The plan starts with ideas for breakfasts and lunches designed to fit your busy schedule, and follows with a day-by-day set of menus that mix these breakfasts and lunches with inspiring but easy-to-cook dinners.

• Each day's menus total 1500-1600 calories. For most people, this level will constitute a weight-loss diet. Once you've achieved your weight goal, check out our "Extras" in the Bonus Pages section, for snacks and additions you may enjoy.

• We have not included "nutritionals" detailing the calories, fat, sodium, etc. for each day. All our recipes are healthy, and when you eat plenty of fresh vegetables, fruits, and whole grains in reasonable portion sizes, you don't need to obsess about numbers. How much more enjoyable to focus on the tastes of your meal, than on the calories and grams of this or that! However, we've included nutritional analyses in our Bonus Pages (page 76), for health professionals or others who may need them.

BREAKFAST 1-2-3 PLAN

A Healthy Start

Eating breakfast starts the day off right.* A good breakfast includes whole grains, and fruit, along with eggs, milk, or yogurt or some other source of protein. Use this 1-2-3 plan to build your own healthy breakfast. Choose one item from each category (1-2-3) every day.

1 For your whole grains, you could pick one bread and one spread:

Bread (1-2 ounces)	**Spread (1-2 tablespoons)**
Whole grain toast	Peanut (or any nut) butter
Whole grain bagel	Hummus
Whole grain pita	Soft cheese
Whole grain English muffin	Guacamole

Or, eat cereal. Enjoy your whole grains in the form of oatmeal or your favorite cold whole grain cereal, about ½ to 1 cup, with about the same amount of milk, yogurt, or soy or nut milk.

2 Pick your favorite fruit–a small to medium whole fruit, or about ½ to 1 cup cut up fruit. Actual fruit will satisfy you better than fruit juice. Pick your favorites, according to the season!

Apples	Cherries	Mango	Peaches
Bananas	Figs	Melon	Pears
Berries	Grapes	Oranges	Pineapple

3 Add an egg, yogurt, or a handful of nuts to help your breakfast stick with you until lunch time. Some quick ideas:

Walnuts, almonds or other nuts – as many as can fit in your cupped hand
Yogurt – buy plain Greek or regular, and add your own fruit or flavorings
Hard-cooked eggs – make several ahead, to last the week
Lowfat milk, or soy or nut milk – on its own, or with your cereal
Soft-cooked or scrambled egg – surprisingly quick

Coffee, tea, or water top off the meal.

*When you skip breakfast, your body says, "Uh oh. Food's scarce. Better slow down the metabolism." Then your body holds onto every calorie you eat all day, making it harder to maintain a sensible weight.

BREAKFAST IDEAS

Weekends

For weekends (or other days when you're not so rushed), we've included suggestions that are a bit more elaborate, such as one of these choices:

- Breakfast Wrap (Day 3)
- Veggie Omelet (Day 7)
- Mediterranean Scramble (Day 16)

Remember, breakfast doesn't have to be limited to traditional breakfast foods. If you want to warm up some soup, or enjoy a big plate of roasted vegetables for breakfast, be our guest!

Grain Leftovers

Here's one idea: If you have extra grains (bulgur, farro, brown rice or any other whole grain) left over from dinner, warm them up with a little milk, cinnamon, honey, and fruit. You'll find it makes an unexpectedly delicious and satisfying breakfast.

LUNCH IDEAS

For lunch, most of our menus feature leftovers and three Mediterranean standbys: salads, wraps or stuffed pitas, and soups.

Salads

You've got a treat in store as you explore the universe of Mediterranean-style salads!

Green Salads: Green salads feature dark, leafy greens like romaine, arugula and mâche, but you can substitute whatever is available. Baby spinach is good, for instance. Add a few chopped vegetables and some nuts, peanuts or seeds, and toss with a delicious vinaigrette.

Grain Salads: Mix a half-cup of leftover cooked whole grains—any variety—with your favorite chopped vegetables or leftover roasted vegetables, then toss with a light vinaigrette. Grain salads are great for lunch at work, because they don't get soggy before noon.

Pasta Salads: Leftover pasta can also serve as the base for a quick salad. It's especially tasty mixed with chopped vegetables, canned tuna, and an herb vinaigrette.

Nuts, peanuts, seeds (sunflower, pumpkin, etc.) and beans add flavor accents and stick-with-you protein to your favorite salads.

Wraps or Stuffed Pitas

Wraps can be made with any kind of whole grain flat bread, including lavaash and tortillas. A round of whole wheat pita bread, cut in half, makes the perfect pocket to hold just about any filling. Some ideas you'll find in our menus include:

- Fresh Vegetable Wrap (Day 1)
- Spinach-Orzo Salad (Day 19)
- Tomato-Goat Cheese Wrap (Day 20)
- Mediterranean Chicken Wrap (Day 21)
- Tuna Wrap (Day 23)

LUNCH IDEAS

Soups

Home-made soups offer more taste and less sodium than store-bought ones. Make a batch on the weekend, and freeze in single-serving portions. Before long you'll have a "soup factory" in your freezer: just grab a container as you head out the door, and warm your soup up in the microwave at work.

Some of the soup recipes we've included here are:

- Lentil Soup (Day 3)
- Minestrone (Day 9)
- Spicy Carrot-Ginger Soup (Day 11)
- Ten-Minute Seafood Stew (Day 19)

Your Own Meze Plate at Work

In Eastern Mediterranean countries, people often enjoy a meze plate—a collection of small bites. If you have a breakroom fridge at work, stock it with a container of olives, some hummus, some cheese and make your own meze plate for lunch. (See Day 6)

Enjoy Leftovers

Most of our recipes make enough for four people. If you don't have four people in your household, then you'll have leftovers you can take to work the next day for lunch or reheat for another dinner. If you think you'll have no leftovers, double your dinner recipe.

Put one serving in a leak-proof leftover container as you clean up the kitchen after dinner, and you'll be ready to race out the door without any extra lunch preparation the next morning.

DAY 1

Breakfast **1** whole grains **2** fruit **3** protein

1 2 slices whole wheat toast with 1 tablespoon peanut butter

2 1 cup sliced cherries

3 6 ounces Greek yogurt

Coffee or tea (1 cup)

(optional milk/sugar)

Lunch

Fresh Vegetable Wrap

1 cup grapes

Iced tea or water

Dinner

Spicy Salmon

Cooked farro

Roasted asparagus with lemon juice and olive oil

Green salad with **Vinaigrette** (page 70)

Dessert: Pears

When you're eating, just eat. Turn off the phone, computer, and television. Play your favorite music on low. Light the candles at dinnertime. Enjoy your friends and family, or the pleasure of your own company. And most of all, enjoy the taste of every bite.

RECIPES

Fresh Vegetable Wrap   Serves 1

Wrap in aluminum foil for easy lunchtime transporting.

1 whole-grain wrap
2 tablespoons hummus (any flavor)
1/2 cup chopped romaine lettuce or
   baby spinach
2 tablespoons diced walnuts
1 small red pepper, seeded and sliced

Place the wrap on a flat surface. Spread the
hummus evenly over the wrap, leaving about
½-inch of space all around the edges. Add
the lettuce, walnuts, and pepper. Wrap tightly,
tucking in the edges.

Spicy Salmon   Serves 4

You can, of course, use this fragrant marinade with just about any kind of
seafood, but the flavors work especially well with salmon. Include one cup of
cooked farro or brown rice (page 73) per serving.

4 cloves garlic, chopped
½ teaspoon sea salt
1 teaspoon crushed red chili pepper
2 tablespoons extra-virgin olive oil
Juice of 1 lemon
4 salmon steaks, each about 4 ounces

Crush the garlic with the salt in a mortar or mash it with a fork in a small
bowl. Add the chili pepper, olive oil, and lemon juice and continue mash-
ing to form a smooth paste. Arrange the fish in a baking dish and spread
the marinade on top. Cover with plastic wrap and refrigerate for up to two
hours. Preheat the oven to 450°F. Uncover the fish and bake for about 20
minutes, or until the fish flakes easily with a fork.

DAY 2

Breakfast ❶ whole grains ❷ fruit ❸ protein

❶❸ 1 cup oatmeal with ½ cup milk, 1 teaspoon honey, and
1 tablespoon almonds

❷ 1 medium banana

Coffee or tea (optional milk/sugar)

Lunch

Fattoush

Or Leftovers: Mix any leftover **Spicy Salmon** from Day 1 dinner with a
little hummus and spread on a slice of whole grain bread. Top with
arugula.

1 cup chopped mango

Iced tea or water

Dinner

Chicken with White Beans

Whole wheat couscous

Cucumber salad with **Herb Vinaigrette** (page 70)

Dessert: Fresh berries

RECIPES

Fattoush   Serves 2

This simple yet tasty salad uses torn pita bread as a main ingredient. It's a great way to use up bread that's just starting to get stale.

2 cups Romaine lettuce
3 radishes, chopped
2 scallions, chopped
1 medium tomato, chopped
1 small cucumber, chopped
¼ cup chopped parsley

1 small green pepper, chopped
1 pita bread
2 teaspoons lemon juice
1 tablespoon extra-virgin olive oil
¼ cup crumbled feta cheese

Combine the lettuce, radishes, scallions, tomato, cucumber, parsley, and green pepper in a bowl and toss gently. Tear the pita into small bits, add to the salad, and toss again. Sprinkle the salad with lemon juice and olive oil, toss, and garnish with the feta cheese.

Chicken with White Beans   Serves 4

This chili-like dish provides plenty of protein and delicious flavor. Include 1 cup of cooked whole wheat couscous per serving (page 73).

1 tablespoon extra-virgin olive oil
1 medium onion
3 cloves garlic, minced
2 teaspoons ground cumin
1 (4.5-ounce) can chopped green chilies, drained
1 (15-ounce) can cannellini beans, rinsed and drained

1 (14.5-ounce) can diced tomatoes, with juice
2 skinless, boneless chicken breasts, cut into 1-inch pieces
Salt and pepper

Heat the oil in a large pot over medium heat. Add the onion and garlic and sauté for about 3 minutes. Add the cumin and cook, stirring for 1 minute. Add the chilies, beans, tomatoes, and chicken and simmer for about 10 minutes. Season with salt and pepper.

DAY 3

Breakfast ❶ whole grains ❷ fruit ❸ protein

❶❸ **Breakfast Wrap:** 1 scrambled egg, ½ cup cooked beans,
1 tablespoon **Guacamole** and 2 tablespoons grated Monterey Jack
cheese or Swiss cheese wrapped in 1 whole wheat tortilla

❷ 1 cup sliced strawberries

Coffee or tea

(optional milk/sugar)

Lunch

Lentil Soup

Or Leftover: Reheat any leftover **Chicken with White Beans** from
Day 2 dinner.

Whole grain pita

Mixed green salad with **Yogurt-Herb Dressing** (page 70)

Dinner

Mediterranean Pita Pizza (page 69)

Green salad with tomatoes, chickpeas,
and cucumbers with **Lemon
Herb Vinaigrette** (page 70)

Dessert: Grapes

Guacamole
Makes 2/3 cup

Use this classic dip as a spread on toast or in wraps. Leftovers will keep for two days, tightly covered, in the refrigerator. To spice it up a bit, add hot peppers or smoked paprika to taste.

1 ripe avocado
1 tablespoon fresh lemon juice
¼ teaspoon salt
2 scallions, minced
4 cherry tomatoes, finely chopped

Cut the avocado in half, remove the seed, and scoop the flesh into a shallow bowl. Add the remaining ingredients and mash with a fork until well blended.

Lentil Soup
Serves 4

You can make this soup with any kind of lentils. If you use red lentils, it will have a lovely orange color. For a protein boost, serve each portion topped with a diced hard-cooked egg.

2 tablespoons extra-virgin olive oil
1 large onion, chopped
1 stalk celery, chopped
1 garlic clove, minced
2 teaspoons ground cumin
2 tablespoons tomato paste

1 quart vegetable or chicken stock
1 cup lentils
Juice of 1 lemon
Salt and pepper
Crumbled feta cheese for garnish

Heat the olive oil in a large pot, add the onion, celery, and garlic, and sauté for 2 minutes. Add the cumin and cook, stirring, for one minute longer. Add the tomato paste, stir until smooth, and add the stock and lentils. Bring just to a boil, reduce the heat, and simmer, partially covered, for 20 minutes, or until the lentils are very soft. Add 1 cup of water if the soup seems too thick. Puree in batches in a food processor or blender, return to the pot, and stir in the lemon juice. Season with salt and pepper. Serve garnished with feta cheese.

DAY 4

Breakfast ❶ whole grains ❷ fruit ❸ protein

❶ 1 whole wheat English muffin with 2 slices of tomato and
   1 tablespoon **Guacamole** (page 19)

❷ 1 cup melon cubes

❸ 1 soft-boiled egg

   Coffee or tea

   (optional milk/sugar)

Lunch

Baby Spinach with Feta and Almonds with **Lemon Vinaigrette**

1 whole grain roll with 1 tablespoon hummus

1 apple

Dinner

Pasta with Fresh Tomatoes

Mixed green salad with Parmesan cheese and **Honey-Mustard
   Vinaigrette** (page 70)

Dessert: Raspberry sorbet

Substitute half an avocado,
mashed, for butter and jelly
on toast.

Baby Spinach with Feta and Almonds   Serves 4

You can use Boston lettuce or delicate, delicious mâche instead of spinach for this refreshing and festive salad.

5 ounces baby spinach
½ cup smoked almonds, coarsely chopped

½ cup crumbled, herbed Feta cheese
¼ cup **Lemon Vinaigrette** (page 70)

Arrange the spinach in a salad bowl. Add the smoked almonds, and feta. Drizzle with dressing, toss gently, and serve.

Pasta with Fresh Tomatoes   Serves 4

Salting the tomatoes ahead of time releases flavor compounds and creates a rich "sauce." Once you allow time for the juices to accumulate, you can then make this easy recipe in less than 15 minutes.

1 pound cherry tomatoes
1 tablespoon extra-virgin olive oil
8 ounces whole wheat penne
Salt and pepper

Cut the tomatoes into halves and put them in a glass or stainless steel bowl. Add the olive oil and the salt. Toss, cover, and leave at room temperature for several hours or overnight, tossing once or twice.

When you're ready to eat, bring a large pot of salted water to a boil. Add the penne and cook according to the package directions. Drain and return the hot pasta to the pan along with the tomatoes and their juice. Toss. Season to taste and serve hot or at room temperature.

Variations:
• If you have some fresh local tomatoes, by all means use about three or four to make the sauce. But the new cherry tomato varieties, including colorful heirlooms and yellow pear, provide plenty of flavor.

• Add ½ cup of chopped fresh basil and top the pasta with a dusting of Parmesan cheese.

DAY 5

Breakfast ① whole grains ② fruit ③ protein

①③ ½ cup whole grain cereal with 1 tablespoon almonds and ½ cup 1% milk

② 1 cup berries

Coffee or tea

(optional milk/sugar)

Lunch

Mediterranean Salad with **Balsamic Vinaigrette**

1 slice whole grain toast or baguette

Or Leftovers: Reheat leftover **Pasta with Fresh Tomatoes** from Day 4 dinner

Dinner

Roasted Vegetable Wraps

Dessert: Melon

Mediterranean Salad   Serves 1

Here's a delicious way to use leftover cooked vegetables and seafood.

½ cup diced cooked new potatoes
1 medium carrot, grated
1 cup cooked green beans
¼ cup cooked fish, shrimp or drained, canned tuna
1 hard-cooked egg
1 cup shredded romaine lettuce
1 tablespoon **Balsamic Vinaigrette** (page 70)

Combine all ingredients and toss gently.

Roasted Vegetable Wraps   Serves 4

Experiment with other vegetables, such as onions, mushrooms, and summer squash, to determine the best time to add them to the mix. Serve leftovers in salad.

2 carrots, peeled and sliced on the diagonal
1 sweet potato, peeled and chopped
1 small winter squash, peeled and chopped
3 tablespoons extra-virgin olive oil
2 red bell peppers, cored, seeded, and chopped
Salt and pepper
4 whole grain wraps

Heat the oven to 425°F. Arrange the carrots, sweet potato, and squash on a baking sheet and drizzle with 2 tablespoons of the olive oil. Bake for 10 minutes. Turn with a spatula. Add the peppers and drizzle with the remaining tablespoon of olive oil. Bake for 10 minutes longer, or until all the vegetables are fork tender. Season with salt and pepper. Lay a wrap out on the counter, spoon on some vegetables, roll up and enjoy.

DAY 6

Breakfast ❶ whole grains ❷ fruit ❸ protein

❶ 2 small oat muffins

❷ 1 banana

❸ 6 ounces Greek yogurt

Coffee or tea

(optional milk/sugar)

Lunch

Meze Plate: 2 tablespoons each of hummus, tabbouleh, and tzatziki, 2 tablespoons olives, and 1 small whole wheat pita

1 cup mixed greens with **Avocado Dressing** (page 70)

Iced tea or water

Dinner

Sirloin Ribbons

Peas

French Potato Salad

Dessert: Blueberry Sorbet

Sirloin Ribbons   Serves 4

Use wooden skewers about 8 inches long for this quick-cooking recipe. Thread the meat by forming an S-shape (sort of like putting a worm on a hook), piercing it every two inches or so with the skewer.

1 pound sirloin steak
1 tablespoon extra-virgin olive oil
1 tablespoon wine vinegar
3 cloves garlic, mashed
2 teaspoons dried oregano

Slice the steak lengthwise into ¼-inch thick strips. Combine the olive oil, vinegar, garlic, and oregano in a flat baking dish and stir with a whisk to mix. Add the steak strips and toss with a fork to coat both sides with the mixture. Refrigerate for about 2 hours. Heat a grill to 350°F or preheat the oven broiler. Thread several slices of meat onto each skewer. Arrange the skewers on the grill or in a broiler pan and cook for about 3 minutes per side, just until the meat is browned. Transfer the skewers to a serving platter.

French Potato Salad   Serves 6

The key to this delicious salad is adding the dressing while the potatoes are still warm. Leave the potatoes unpeeled if you wish.

6-8 medium yellow potatoes
2 tablespoons extra-virgin olive oil
1 tablespoon Dijon mustard
1 teaspoon dried tarragon
Salt and pepper

Cook the potatoes in a large pot of boiling water until they can be easily pierced with a knife. Drain and let cool slightly. Combine the olive oil and mustard in small bowl. When the potatoes are cool enough to handle but still warm, chop them into a large bowl. Add the dressing and toss to coat. Add the tarragon and season with salt and pepper. Serve warm or cold.

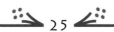

DAY 7

Breakfast ❶ whole grains ❷ fruit ❸ protein

❶❸ 6 ounces Greek yogurt with ¼ cup granola

❷ 1 banana

   1 cup grapefruit juice

   Coffee or tea

   (optional milk/sugar)

Lunch

Veggie Omelet

Salad: 1 cup baby spinach with ½ cup sliced strawberries,
   1 tablespoon walnuts, and 1 tablespoon goat cheese with
   Herb Vinaigrette (page 70)

Dinner

Six-Minute Shrimp

Whole wheat linguini

Green beans

Arugula, cherry tomato, and cucumber salad with **Vinaigrette**
   (page 70)

Dessert: Fresh figs

Veggie Omelet   Serves 2

You can also add onions, yellow squash, or leftover cooked vegetables.

1 tablespoon extra-virgin olive oil   1 teaspoon dried tarragon
1 small zucchini, diced   2 eggs
1 red or orange bell pepper, diced   2 teaspoons water

Heat the olive oil in a small skillet. Add the zucchini and pepper and sauté over medium-low heat for about 5 minutes, until the vegetables soften. Turn the heat up to medium high and cook for a few minutes until the liquid in the pan evaporates. Combine the tarragon, eggs, and water in a small bowl and beat until smooth. Pour the eggs into the pan on top of the vegetables, reduce the heat to medium low, and cook until the edges of the omelet are set. Gently run a spatula under the eggs, lift up and tilt the pan to let some of the uncooked egg run into the bottom. Continue cooking for about 3 minutes longer, until the eggs are set.

Six-Minute Shrimp   Serves 4

Here's a very easy way to cook shrimp, whether fresh or frozen. Include 1 cup of cooked, whole wheat linguini per serving.

2 tablespoons extra-virgin olive oil
2 cloves garlic, chopped
1 onion, sliced
1 pound fresh shrimp (about 25), peeled, or 1 pound frozen shrimp, thawed for 5 minutes in cold water
1 teaspoon dried thyme
Salt and pepper

Arrange the oven rack so it is about 8 inches from the heat source. Heat the broiler. Heat the olive oil in a large cast iron or ovenproof skillet. Add the garlic and onion and cook over medium heat for about three minutes. Add the shrimp, sprinkle with the thyme, season with salt and pepper and toss gently to mix evenly. Place the pan under the broiler and cook for about 3 minutes; stir and cook for another 3 minutes, or until the shrimp turn pink.

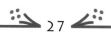

DAY 8

Breakfast ❶ whole grains ❷ fruit ❸ protein

❶ 1 cup oatmeal with 1 tablespoon almonds
and 1 tablespoon raisins

❷ 1 cup sliced peaches

❸ 6 ounces Greek yogurt

Coffee or tea

(optional milk/sugar)

Lunch

Greek Salad

1 whole wheat pita

Dinner

Cauliflower with Chickpeas

Whole wheat couscous

Mixed green salad with **Yogurt-Herb Dressing** (page 70)

Dessert: Fresh pineapple

After meals, go for a relaxing walk—
*like the Italians with their **passeggiata** or*
*the Spaniards with their **paseo**.*

Greek Salad   Serves 1

Add cucumbers and up to ½ cup cooked lentils to this classic salad if you wish.

2 cups chopped romaine
  lettuce
1 medium tomato, diced
4 pitted Greek, kalamata,
  or any cured black olives
2 tablespoons chopped parsley
  (optional)
Dried oregano to taste
1 tablespoon crumbled
  feta cheese
1 tablespoon **Balsamic
  Vinaigrette** (page 70)

Combine all the ingredients and toss gently.

Cauliflower with Chickpeas   Serves 4

Add a can of tuna to this quick dish, or substitute broccoli for the cauliflower. Include 1 cup of cooked whole wheat couscous per serving (page 73).

2 tablespoons extra-virgin olive oil
1 onion, chopped
1 yellow squash, chopped
1 red pepper, seeded and chopped
1 small head cauliflower, broken
  into florets

1 teaspoon cumin
1 (14.5-ounce) can diced tomatoes
1 (15-ounces) can chickpeas,
  drained and rinsed

Heat the olive oil in a large pot over medium heat. Add the onion, squash, and pepper and sauté for about 5 minutes, until the vegetables soften. Add the cauliflower and cook for 5 minutes longer. Sprinkle in the cumin and cook for 1 minute. Add the tomatoes and chickpeas, stir, and cook for 5 minutes longer, or until the cauliflower is tender.

DAY 9

Breakfast ❶ whole grains ❷ fruit ❸ protein

❶ 1 slice whole wheat toast

❷ 1 orange

❸ 1 soft-boiled egg

 1 small tomato, sliced

 Coffee or tea

 (optional milk/sugar)

Lunch

Minestrone

Or Leftovers: Reheat leftover **Cauliflower and Chickpeas** from Day 8 dinner.

1 whole-grain pita bread

1 apple

Iced tea or water

Dinner

Mussels Provençal

Whole grain linguini

Mixed green salad with **Lemon Vinaigrette** (page 70)

Dessert: Raspberries

Minestrone   Serves 6

Make your own soup for the very best flavor, and for lower sodium. Add a sprinkling of grated Parmesan on top.

2 tablespoons extra-virgin olive oil
1 yellow onion, diced
2 carrots, peeled and chopped
2 stalks celery, chopped
2-3 cloves garlic, minced
1 pound spinach, chopped
1 large potato, peeled and chopped
1 (14.5-ounce) can diced
   tomatoes, with juice

2 teaspoons dried rosemary
4 cups chicken stock
¼ cup small dried pasta
1 (15-ounce) can cannellini beans,
   drained and rinsed
Salt and pepper

Heat the olive oil over medium heat in a large pot. Add the onion, carrots, celery, and garlic and sauté for about 5 minutes, until the vegetables soften. Add the spinach and potato and sauté for 2 minutes longer. Add the tomatoes and rosemary and simmer for about 5 minutes, until the spinach is wilted. Add the stock and bring to a boil. Add the pasta, reduce the heat to medium and cook until the potato and pasta are tender, about 10 minutes. Stir in the beans and simmer for 5 minutes. Season with salt and pepper.

Mussels Provençal   Serves 4

Mussels are easy to cook, and they're one of the most sustainable of seafood choices. Include 1 cup of cooked, whole grain linguini per serving.

3 pounds mussels
1 cup dry white wine
2 cloves garlic, finely minced
1 small onion, diced

1 stalk celery, diced
1 large tomato, diced
Salt and pepper

Soak the mussels in cold water and scrub to remove any dirt. Remove any hairy "beards" with a sharp knife. Drain. Combine the wine, garlic, onions, celery and tomato in a large pot and bring just to a boil over high heat. Add the mussels, cover, reduce the heat to medium, and cook for about 10 minutes, until the mussels have opened. Using tongs, transfer the mussels to large bowls (discard any that have not opened) along with the linguini. Strain the broth remaining in the pan into a saucepan and boil for about 3 minutes. Season with salt and pepper, and pour the broth over the mussels.

DAY 10

Breakfast ❶ whole grains ❷ fruit ❸ protein

❶ ❸ 1 slice cinnamon-raisin bread with 1 tablespoon goat cheese

❷ 4 small fresh figs

1 cup freshly squeezed orange juice

Coffee or tea

(optional milk/sugar)

Lunch

Citrus Salad

1 medium whole grain pita with 2 tablespoons **Bean Dip** (page 61)

Dinner

Oven-Roasted Pork Tenderloin

Whole wheat couscous

Green beans

Green salad with **Herb Vinaigrette** (page 70)

Dessert: Orange Sorbet

Citrus Salad   Serves 1

For a different flavor, substitute grapefruit sections for the orange or use a few of each. You can also swap diced walnuts or almonds for the peanuts.

1 cup baby spinach leaves
1 orange, peeled and sectioned
½ avocado, peeled and diced
2 slices red onion
2 tablespoons peanuts, crushed
1 tablespoon **Lemon Vinaigrette** (page 70)

Arrange the spinach on a plate or in a shallow salad bowl. Top with the orange, avocado, onion, and peanuts, and drizzle on the dressing.

Oven-Roasted Pork Tenderloin   Serves 4

Buy a pork tenderloin, not a pork "loin," to make this 20-minute meal. Leftovers are delicious in wraps. Include 1 cup of cooked whole wheat couscous per serving (page 73).

1 pork tenderloin, about 1 pound
1 tablespoon Dijon mustard
2 cloves garlic, minced
1 tablespoon extra-virgin olive oil
1 teaspoon dried oregano
1 teaspoon dried rosemary
Salt and pepper

Preheat the oven to 450°F. Put the pork in a shallow roasting pan. Spread the mustard over the top. In a small bowl combine the garlic, olive oil, oregano, rosemary, salt and pepper. Mix with a spoon and spread on top of the mustard layer. Roast the pork for 10 minutes. Turn over and roast for another 10 minutes, or until it registers 155°F on an instant-read thermometer. Remove to a cutting board and slice on the diagonal.

DAY 11

Breakfast ❶ whole grains ❷ fruit ❸ protein

❶ 1 slice whole wheat toast

❷ 1 cup blueberries

❸ 1 egg, scrambled in 1 tablespoon olive oil with 1 small tomato, and ½ ounce crumbled feta cheese

Coffee or tea

(optional milk/sugar)

Lunch

Spicy Carrot-Ginger Soup

1 whole wheat pita stuffed with ½ avocado, 4 pitted kalamata olives, and 2 tablespoons hummus

Or Leftovers: Slice leftover **Oven-Roasted Pork Tenderloin** from Day 10 dinner and use in a whole grain pita with hummus and sliced apples.

Dinner

Honey-Mustard Chicken and Vegetables

Mixed green salad with cucumber and tomato with **Avocado Dressing** (page 70)

Dessert: Greek yogurt with honey and walnuts

Spicy Carrot-Ginger Soup   Serves 10

Allowing the carrots to cook slowly helps them caramelize and become sweeter. Serve with a dollop of plain Greek yogurt on top.

2 tablespoons extra-virgin olive oil
1 small yellow onion, chopped
1-2 teaspoons cumin seed
½ teaspoon cayenne
3 pounds carrots, peeled and
   roughly chopped
4 cloves garlic, minced

2 tablespoons minced fresh ginger
4 cups chicken or vegetable stock
Salt
Plain Greek yogurt (optional)

Heat the olive oil in a large pot over medium high heat and sauté the onion for 2 to 3 minutes. Stir in the cumin seed and cayenne. Stir in the carrots. Reduce the heat to low and cook, covered, for 7 to 8 minutes, stirring once or twice. Add the garlic and ginger and increase the heat to medium high, stirring well. Cook for another 1 to 2 minutes. Add the chicken stock and bring to a boil. Cover, reduce the heat to low, and simmer until the carrots are fork-tender, about 10 to 15 minutes. Puree the soup in batches in a food processor until smooth. Season with salt and serve hot.

Honey-Mustard Chicken and Vegetables   Serves 4

This meal-in-one is a great choice for beginning cooks. And thanks to the foil packaging, cleanup is a breeze.

1 pound boneless skinless chicken
   breasts, sliced
1 pound Yukon Gold potatoes,
   thinly sliced
1 medium onion, sliced
1 zucchini, sliced
1 red or yellow bell pepper, sliced

Honey-Mustard Vinaigrette
(page 70)
4 teaspoons dried oregano or
   Italian herb blend
Salt and pepper

Preheat the oven to 400°F or heat a grill. Combine all the ingredients in a large bowl. Arrange 4 large squares of heavy-duty aluminum foil on the counter and lightly grease each square. Place ¼ of the ingredients in the center of each square. Fold the top and the sides of each square to enclose the filling, leaving some space within the packet for air to circulate. Arrange the packets on a baking sheet and bake for 30 minutes or grill over medium heat for about 25 to 30 minutes, until the chicken is cooked through and the potatoes are soft. Carefully open the packets and transfer the contents to serving plates.

DAY 12

Breakfast ❶ whole grains ❷ fruit ❸ protein

❶ 1 cup whole grain cereal

❷ 1 cup strawberries

❸ ½ cup 1% milk

Coffee or tea

(optional milk/sugar)

Lunch

Turkey-Apple-Spinach Salad with **Honey-Mustard Vinaigrette**

1 small whole wheat pita

2 tablespoons hummus

Dinner

North African Vegetable Curry

Barley

Baby spinach, tomato, and feta salad with **Vinaigrette** (page 70)

Dessert: Peaches

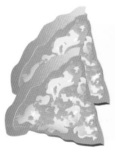

Take a 10 to 15 minute break before you help yourself to seconds—particularly if you were voracious before the meal. Oftentimes our stomachs are full before our brain is, and the wait helps to ascertain if you are satisfied.

Turkey-Apple-Spinach Salad   Serves 1

You can make this tasty lunch in minutes. Add 2 tablespoons of chopped walnuts if you wish.

2 cups baby spinach leaves
2 ounces smoked turkey, sliced or chopped
1 ounce Swiss cheese, diced
1 small apple, diced
1 stalk celery, diced
1 tablespoon **Honey-Mustard Vinaigrette** (page 70)

Arrange the spinach on a salad plate. Top with the turkey, cheese, apple, and celery, and drizzle on the dressing.

North African Vegetable Curry   Serves 4

Here's an easy way to discover the haunting flavors of a Mediterranean curry. Include 1 cup of cooked barley per serving (page 73).

1 tablespoon extra-virgin olive oil
1 onion, diced
3 cloves garlic, diced
2 stalks celery, chopped
2 carrots, chopped
1 zucchini, chopped
1 sweet potato, peeled and diced

2 teaspoons curry powder
1 teaspoon cumin
1 (15.5-ounce) can diced tomatoes with juice
1 cup light coconut milk
Salt and pepper

Heat the olive oil in a large pot over medium heat. Add the onion, garlic, celery, and carrots and cook, stirring once or twice, for about 5 minutes, until the vegetables soften.

Add the zucchini and sweet potato and cook for 3 minutes. Sprinkle the curry powder and cumin over the vegetables and toss to coat, cooking for about 1 minute longer. Add the tomatoes and coconut milk, stir, cover, reduce the heat to low, and cook for 15 minutes, or until the sweet potato is soft. Season to taste with salt and pepper

DAY 13

Breakfast ❶ whole grains ❷ fruit ❸ protein

❶ 1 slice whole-wheat toast

❷ 1 medium orange

❸ 1 soft-boiled egg

  Coffee or tea

  (optional milk/sugar)

Lunch

Mushroom Pita

1 cup grapes

Dinner

Salmon Kebabs

Brown rice

Arugula salad with **Avocado Dressing** (page 70)

Dessert: Strawberries

Mushroom Pita   Serves 1

If you bring your lunch to work or school, pack the marinated mushrooms in a separate container and assemble your pita just before eating so your sandwich won't get soggy.

½ cup sliced mushrooms
2 teaspoons extra-virgin olive oil
1 teaspoon balsamic vinegar
1 tablespoon diced olives
2 scallions, chopped

1 garlic clove, minced
Romaine lettuce
½ whole wheat pita
1 tablespoon crumbled goat cheese

Combine the mushrooms, olive oil, vinegar, olives, scallions, and garlic in a small bowl and toss to blend. Cover and refrigerate for one hour. To serve, place the lettuce in the pita half, fill with the mushroom mixture and the goat cheese.

Salmon Kebabs   Serves 4

Here's a great way to make dinner in 30 minutes. Add a few cherry tomatoes if you wish. Include one cup of cooked brown rice per serving (page 73).

Juice of 1 lime
1 garlic clove, minced
2 tablespoons extra-virgin olive oil
2 teaspoons Dijon mustard
1 tablespoon chopped fresh
   tarragon or 1 teaspoon dried

1 pound salmon fillet
1 medium zucchini
1 large onion
1 red, yellow or orange bell pepper

Combine the lime juice, garlic, olive oil, mustard, and tarragon in a bowl and blend with a whisk. Cut the remaining ingredients into chunks, add to the bowl, and toss gently to coat. Set aside for 15 minutes.

Preheat the grill or broiler. Thread the salmon, zucchini, onion, and pepper chunks onto four skewers. If using the broiler, arrange the skewers in a baking dish. Broil or grill for 5 minutes. Turn and cook for 5 minutes longer.

DAY 14

Breakfast ❶ whole grains ❷ fruit ❸ protein

❶ 1 cup whole grain cereal

❷ 1 cup melon chunks

❸ ½ cup 1% milk

Coffee or tea

(optional milk/sugar)

Lunch

Open-Face Tuna Sandwich: 1 slice rye bread topped with
½ cup tuna mixed with 1 tablespoon Greek yogurt,
topped with 2 slices of tomato

1 cup sliced peaches

4 whole grain crackers

Dinner

Pasta with Spinach and Beans

Mixed green salad with tomatoes, whole grain croutons and
Honey-Mustard Vinaigrette (page 70)

Dessert: Cherries

Tips for eating out: *Order
a second appetizer as a main
course, or share a dessert.*

Pasta with Spinach and Beans   Serves 4

This winning combination provides a complete meal in one bowl. It comes together quickly, so have all the ingredients prepared and ready for the last-minute combining.

12 ounces whole wheat rotini or ziti
2 tablespoons extra-virgin olive oil
2 cloves garlic, minced
1 (15-ounce) can cannellini beans, rinsed and drained
4 cups chopped baby spinach leaves
½ cup (2 ounces) grated Parmesan cheese
Salt and pepper

Cook the pasta in boiling water according to the package directions. While the pasta is cooking, heat the olive oil in a skillet and sauté the garlic over medium heat for 3 minutes, stirring frequently. Add the beans, reduce the heat to low, and cook, stirring occasionally, until the pasta is ready. Drain the pasta in a colander in the sink and immediately put the spinach in the bottom of the hot pasta pot. Pour the drained pasta on top, add the beans and garlic, and sprinkle with the cheese. Cover and let the mixture sit for 2 minutes. Turn out into a large serving bowl, season with salt and pepper, toss, and serve.

DAY 15

Breakfast ❶ whole grains ❷ fruit ❸ protein

❶ 2 small whole grain muffins

❷ 1 cup blueberries

❸ 6 ounces Greek yogurt

Coffee or tea

(optional milk/sugar)

Lunch

Shrimp Salad

2 whole grain crackers

Dinner

Spinach-Mushroom Strata

Sliced tomatoes

Dessert: Plums

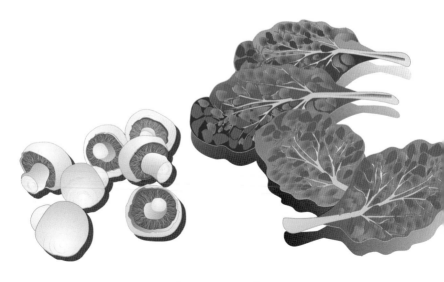

Shrimp Salad   Serves 1

Keep cooked, frozen shrimp in the freezer so you can pull out and thaw a handful anytime to make this tasty salad.

½ cup cooked shrimp
4 scallions, sliced
1 tablespoon **Lemon Vinaigrette** (page 70)

1 cup salad greens
¼ cup whole grain croutons
1 tablespoon Parmesan cheese

Combine the shrimp, scallions, and vinaigrette in a small bowl, toss, and let sit for about 10 minutes. Arrange the greens on a plate or in a shallow bowl, and top with the shrimp, croutons, and cheese.

Spinach-Mushroom Strata   Serves 6

Plan ahead to make this delicious and economical dish, which is a great way to use up bread before it turns stale. Change up the flavor by adding your choice of other sautéed, diced vegetables.

1 (10-ounce) package frozen spinach, thawed
1 tablespoon extra-virgin olive oil
1 cup sliced mushrooms
4 eggs

2 cups 1% milk
1 teaspoon Dijon mustard
6 slices thick, day old whole wheat bread, cut into cubes
1¼ cups grated cheese

Lightly grease a two-quart baking dish and set aside. Squeeze the spinach in your hands over a strainer to remove any moisture. Place it on a cutting board and chop finely. Heat the olive oil in a skillet and sauté the mushrooms for about 4 minutes, until they're soft and beginning to lose moisture. Add the spinach and cook for two minutes longer. Beat the eggs with the milk and mustard.

To assemble, layer half of the bread cubes into the bottom of the baking dish. Top with the mushrooms and spinach, and sprinkle with 1 cup of the cheese. Cover with the remaining bread cubes. Pour the egg mixture over the top and press down gently with a spatula. Sprinkle on the remaining ¼ cup of cheese. Cover with plastic wrap and refrigerate overnight. Preheat the oven to 350°F. Uncover the strata and bake for 30 to 45 minutes, until browned.

DAY 16

Breakfast ❶ whole grains ❷ fruit ❸ protein

❶ 1 slice whole wheat toast with 1 tablespoon jam

❷ 1 orange

❸ **Mediterranean Scramble**

Coffee or tea

(optional milk/sugar)

Lunch

Carrot Peanut Butter Wrap: Spread 1 whole wheat tortilla with
2 tablespoons peanut butter, sprinkle with 1 medium grated carrot
and 2 tablespoons raisins, and roll up. Experiment with other fillings
like grated cabbage, sliced apples, leftover chicken, or substitute
Greek yogurt or hummus for the peanut butter.

1 kiwi

Dinner

Herb-Baked Fish

Bulgur

Sliced cucumbers with **Yogurt-Herb Dressing** (page 70)

Dessert: Watermelon

Build meals around leftovers.
*Prepare more food than you need for
lunches and dinners so you can enjoy
quickly reheated leftovers at work or
on busy days at home.*

Mediterranean Scramble   Serves 4

Make this special egg dish on a weekend or holiday morning.

2 tablespoons extra-virgin olive oil
1 medium onion
1 (14.5-ounce) can diced
   tomatoes, drained
2 cloves garlic, minced

8 large eggs
¼ cup minced cilantro (optional)
Salt and pepper

Heat the oil in a large skillet over medium heat. Add the onion and cook, stirring, until the onion is golden but not browned, about 10 minutes. Add the tomatoes and garlic, and cook for about 5 minutes, until most of the liquid from the tomatoes has evaporated. In a large bowl, combine the eggs, cilantro, salt and pepper and whisk until smooth. Pour the egg mixture into the skillet and cook, stirring gently, until the eggs are set. Serve hot.

Herb-Baked Fish   Serves 4

Get into the habit of serving fish to your family at least twice a week. It's a good source of protein and exposes kids to the world beyond burgers. Include 1 cup of cooked bulgur per serving (page 73).

1 pound fresh halibut, cod, or salmon
2 teaspoons olive oil
1 teaspoon dried thyme
1/4 cup grated Parmesan cheese

Preheat the oven to 425° F. Place the fish in a flat baking dish, skin side down. Rub both sides with olive oil. Sprinkle the top with the thyme and cheese. Bake for 10 minutes, or until the fish flakes easily with a fork. Serve immediately.

DAY 17

Breakfast ❶ whole grains ❷ fruit ❸ protein

❶ 1 slice whole wheat toast with 1 tablespoon peanut butter

❷ 1 cup strawberries

❸ 6 ounces Greek yogurt

Coffee or tea

(optional milk/sugar)

Lunch

Tabbouleh

1 whole grain pita

1 apple

Dinner

Turkey Couscous

Mixed green salad with
Herb Vinaigrette (page 70)

Dessert: Blueberries

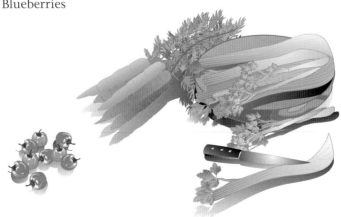

RECIPES

Tabbouleh   Serves 2

Here's a great way to use up fresh parsley. Garnish with feta if you wish, and add diced cucumber, diced celery, or chopped scallions. Bulgur comes in various "grinds" ranging from fine to coarse. The coarser the grind, the more texture your salad will have.

½ cup cooked bulgur (page 73)   ¼ cup chopped mint (optional)
1 tablespoon lemon juice   1 medium tomato, diced
1 garlic clove, minced   Salt and pepper
1 cup chopped parsley

Combine the warm cooked bulgur, lemon juice, and garlic and chill for 30 minutes. Add the remaining ingredients and season with salt and pepper.

Turkey Couscous   Serves 4

Allow time for the turkey to marinate overnight. This dish tastes even better the day after you make it.

1 pound boneless turkey breast,   2 carrots, peeled and chopped
  cut into 1-inch cubes   1 pint cherry tomatoes, cut in
2 tablespoons extra-virgin olive oil   halves
1 tablespoon red wine vinegar   1 (15-ounces) can chickpeas,
1 tablespoon fresh minced   drained and rinsed
  rosemary or 1 teaspoon dried   1 cup whole wheat couscous,
1 large onion, chopped   cooked
2 cloves garlic, minced   ¼ cup raisins
2 stalks celery, chopped

Place the turkey in a large bowl. Add 1 tablespoon of the olive oil, the vinegar, and rosemary and toss to coat all the pieces. Cover and refrigerate overnight or for at least 8 hours. Heat the remaining 1 tablespoon of olive oil in a large pot, and sauté the onion, garlic, celery, and carrots for about 3 minutes, until they just begin to soften. Add the turkey and cook, stirring several times, until no longer pink. Add the tomatoes and chickpeas, stir gently, and simmer for 15 minutes. Prepare the couscous according to the package directions. Add the raisins to the couscous and cook for 1 minute longer. Spoon the couscous into individual serving bowls and top with the turkey mixture.

DAY 18

Breakfast ➊ whole grains ➋ fruit ➌ protein

➊ 1 slice whole wheat toast with 1 tablespoon goat cheese

➋ 1 pear

➌ 1 hard-cooked egg

Coffee or tea

(optional milk/sugar)

Lunch

Open-Face Roasted Vegetable Sandwiches

Lentil Soup (page 19)

Or Leftovers: Reheat leftover **Turkey Couscous** from Day 17 dinner.

Dinner

Cherry Tomato and Olive Pizza

Mixed green salad with **Herb Vinaigrette** (page 70)

Dessert: Lemon Sorbet

Learn to cook with herbs and spices.

Adding cinnamon, cumin, curry powder, and pepper, fresh basil, parsley, and mint, and fresh or dried oregano, thyme, rosemary, tarragon can bring great new flavors to vegetables, grains, and pasta, with no added calories. Try salt-free spice and herb blends, too.

Open-Face Roasted Vegetable Sandwiches   Serves 8

Vegetables cooked at high temperatures become sweeter and softer. Hot, cold, or at room temperature, they make great lunches, easy sandwich ingredients, and colorful additions to grain salads. This recipe makes enough for eight sandwiches. Store leftovers for up to three days in the refrigerator.

2 medium onions, thinly sliced
2 bell peppers, seeded and sliced
8 large mushrooms, sliced
1 medium zucchini, sliced
2 stalks celery, cut on the diagonal
 into 2-inch slices

2 tablespoons extra-virgin olive oil
4 3-inch slices whole grain
 baguette
8 tablespoons hummus
Salt and pepper

Preheat the oven to 450°F. Line a baking sheet with aluminum foil and lightly grease the foil. Arrange the vegetables in a single layer and lightly drizzle with the olive oil. Bake for 10 to 15 minutes, until the vegetables are just starting to darken around the edges. Cut each slice of bread in half lengthwise and spread each piece with hummus. Add about ½ cup of roasted vegetables and season with salt and pepper. Refrigerate any leftover, cooled vegetables in a container with a tight-fitting lid.

Cherry Tomato and Olive Pizza   Serves 4

Add other toppings as you wish. Try roasted peppers or eggplant, artichoke hearts, capers and olives.

1 packaged prebaked whole grain
 flatbread or pizza crust
½ cup plain Greek Yogurt
1 cup red or yellow cherry
 tomatoes, halved

½ cup pitted, halved Kalamata
 olives
3 tablespoons feta cheese
2 teaspoons dried oregano

Preheat the oven to 400°F. Put the crust on a baking sheet. Spread the Greek yogurt evenly over the top. Scatter the tomatoes, olives, and feta cheese over the top and sprinkle with the oregano. Bake for about 10 minutes, until the toppings are sizzling. Cut into slices with a pizza cutter or large knife.

DAY 19

Breakfast ❶ whole grains ❷ fruit ❸ protein

❶ 2 slices whole grain bread baguette with 2 tablespoons fruit preserves

❷ 1 cup melon cubes

❸ 1 slice/ounce Swiss cheese

Coffee or tea

(optional milk/sugar)

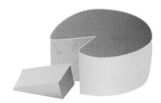

LUNCH

Spinach-Orzo Salad

1 small whole wheat pita

Dinner

Ten-Minute Seafood Stew

Brown rice

Arugula salad with feta cheese and **Vinaigrette** (page 70)

Dessert: Greek yogurt with honey and walnuts

Spinach-Orzo Salad   Serves 1

This salad will keep for three days, tightly covered, in the refrigerator. It tastes best after it has chilled for at least two hours.

½ cup whole wheat or rainbow orzo
1 cup chopped fresh spinach
4 sliced kalamata olives
1 small tomato, diced

2 slices red onion, diced
1 tablespoon crumbed feta cheese
1 tablespoon **Lemon Vinaigrette** (page 70)

Bring 2 cups of water to a boil in a large saucepan, stir in the orzo, and cook for 6 to 8 minutes, until the orzo is tender but still firm to the bite. While the orzo is cooking, combine the spinach, olives, tomato, onion, and feta in a bowl. Toss gently to combine. Drain the orzo and while still hot, pour it on top of the other ingredients. Let sit for several minutes, to slightly wilt the spinach and soften the cheese. Add the dressing and toss. Serve warm, cold, or at room temperature.

Ten-Minute Seafood Stew   Serves 4

Make this quick, easy, and delicious meal with shrimp, scallops, calamari, or any firm-fleshed fish, or a combination of several. Include 1 cup of cooked brown rice per serving (page 73).

1 tablespoon olive oil
2 cloves garlic, minced
1 onion, diced
1 stalk celery, diced
1 (8-ounce) bottle clam juice
2 (14.5-ounce) cans diced tomatoes

1 tablespoon fresh or 1 teaspoon dried thyme
Juice of ½ lemon
1 pound fresh seafood

Heat the oil in a large pot over medium heat. Add the garlic, onion, and celery and sauté for 5 minutes. Add the clam juice, tomatoes, thyme, and lemon juice, increase the heat to high, and bring the stew almost to a boil. Add the seafood, turn the heat down to medium-low, and simmer for 5 minutes until the seafood is cooked. Serve hot, over the rice.

DAY 20

Breakfast ❶ whole grains ❷ fruit ❸ protein

❶ 2 whole grain English muffin halves with 1 tablespoon peanut butter

❷ 1 banana

❸ 6 ounces Greek yogurt

Coffee or tea

(optional milk/sugar)

Lunch

Tomato-Goat Cheese Wrap

Or Leftovers: Reheat leftover **Ten-Minute Seafood Stew** from Day 19 dinner.

Dinner

Chicken Kebabs with Yogurt Sauce

Dessert: Clementines

RECIPES

Tomato-Goat Cheese Wrap   Serves 1

Switch up this quick lunch by substituting popular Mediterranean spreads such as hummus, Greek yogurt, tzatziki, or baba ghanoush for the goat cheese. If it's destined for a lunch box, wrap it tightly in foil.

1 whole grain wrap
2 tablespoons goat cheese
1 small tomato, diced
1 tablespoon diced olives
½ cup baby spinach
1 tablespoon **Balsamic Vinaigrette** (page 70)

Lay the wrap out flat on the counter. Spread it with the goat cheese and sprinkle with the tomato, olives, and spinach. Drizzle on the vinaigrette and roll up.

Chicken Kebabs with Yogurt Sauce   Serves 4

Here's an easy way to cook chicken. Serve the skewers on top of lettuce, along with some whole wheat pita bread and sliced tomatoes.

1 cup plain Greek yogurt
3 cloves garlic, minced
1 tablespoon chopped fresh dill or 1 teaspoon dried
Juice of 1 lemon
1 teaspoon cumin
1 pound boneless, skinless chicken breasts

Combine the yogurt, garlic, dill, lemon juice and cumin in a bowl and stir until smooth. Set aside about half of the sauce. Cut the chicken into 1-inch chunks and add to the bowl with the remaining sauce. Toss and set aside for 10 minutes. Preheat the broiler or heat the grill. Thread the chicken onto skewers and cook for 5 minutes. Turn and cook for another 4 minutes. Serve with sauce on the side.

DAY 21

Breakfast ① whole grains ② fruit ③ protein

① 1 slice whole wheat toast with jam

② 1 cup grapes

③ 1 scrambled egg

Coffee or tea

(optional milk/sugar)

Lunch

Mediterranean Chicken Wrap

1 apple with 2 tablespoons peanut butter

Dinner

Pasta with Avocado Sauce

Mixed green salad with **Balsamic Vinaigrette** (page 70)

Dessert: Oranges

Eat nuts, peanuts, and seeds daily.
Include up to 2 tablespoons of almonds,
walnuts, pistachios, sunflower seeds, and
pumpkin seeds in Greek yogurt, in salads,
or with grains. And when you need a quick
snack, have ¼ cup, or one handful.

Mediterranean Chicken Wrap   Serves 1

You can also enjoy this delicious mixture on top of salad greens.

2 tablespoons plain Greek yogurt
½ teaspoon oregano
1 stalk celery, diced
2 tablespoons chopped walnuts
½ cup chopped cooked chicken
1 cup mixed salad greens

Combine the yogurt and oregano in a small bowl and stir until smooth. Add the celery, walnuts, and chicken (last night's chicken tastes great!) and toss gently until well mixed. Arrange the greens on a plate or in a shallow salad bowl and top with the chicken salad.

Pasta with Avocado Sauce   Serves 6

Use farfalle or any other kind of whole wheat pasta with this delicious, creamy sauce.

1 pound whole wheat farfalle
4 cloves garlic, chopped
3 tablespoons extra-virgin olive oil
Juice of 1 lemon
2 ripe avocados, peeled and pitted
1 small ripe tomato or 4-5 cherry tomatoes, chopped
½ cup chopped fresh basil (optional)
Salt and pepper
Parmesan cheese for garnish (optional)

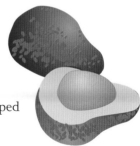

Cook the pasta according to the package directions. While the pasta is cooking, combine the garlic, olive oil, and lemon juice in a food processor and blend until smooth. Add the avocados, tomato, and basil and process until smooth. Season with salt and pepper. Drain the pasta and serve topped with the sauce. Garnish with a bit of Parmesan cheese.

DAY 22

Breakfast ❶ whole grains ❷ fruit ❸ protein

❶ 1 cup oatmeal with ¼ cup walnuts

❷ 2 tablespoons raisins, and 1 diced apple

❸ 6 ounces Greek yogurt

Coffee or tea

(optional milk/sugar)

Lunch

Chickpea-Walnut Salad: 1 cup mixed greens tossed with ½ cup cooked chickpeas, ½ cup corn kernels, ¼ cup walnuts, 1 ounce feta cheese with **Lemon Vinaigrette** (page 70).

Whole wheat pita

1 pear

Dinner

Pasta Shells with Clam Sauce

Green beans

Dessert: Pears

Drink water throughout the day.
Get into the habit of reaching for water with and between meals. Add a squeeze of lemon for extra flavor.

Pasta Shells with Clam Sauce   Serves 6

Here's an easy and delicious sauce that makes use of two pantry staples. Add an 8-ounce bottle of clam juice if you want more sauce.

1 box whole grain pasta shells
2 tablespoons extra-virgin olive oil
4-6 cloves garlic, sliced
2 (6.5-ounce) cans chopped clams
½ to ¾ cup chopped parsley
Juice of ½ lemon
Parmesan cheese (optional)

Cook the pasta according to the package directions. While the pasta is cooking, heat the olive oil in a skillet and sauté the garlic over low heat until softened. Add the clams and juice from the can and warm over low heat for several minutes. Add the parsley and cook for several minutes longer. Squeeze the lemon juice into the sauce and stir. Drain the pasta. Serve the sauce on the cooked pasta, topped with a grating of Parmesan cheese if you wish.

DAY 23

Breakfast ① whole grains ② fruit ③ protein

①③ 1 whole grain bagel with soft cheese

② 1 cup blueberries

1 cup freshly-squeezed orange juice

Coffee or tea

(optional milk/sugar)

Lunch

Tuna Wrap: 1 whole grain tortilla spread with 2 tablespoons plain Greek yogurt, ½ cup drained, flaked canned tuna, ¼ cup slivered almonds, 1 grated carrot, ½ thinly sliced apple, greens, with **Honey-Mustard Vinaigrette** (page 70).

Iced tea or water

Dinner

Vegetable Beef Kebabs

Brown rice

Mixed green salad with **Honey-Mustard Vinaigrette** (page 70)

Dessert: Fresh figs

For a quick dessert, dust one sliced apple with cinnamon and microwave on high for 2 minutes.

Vegetable Beef Kebabs   Serves 4

Pair meat with a number of other vegetables to keep these kebabs heart healthy. Include 1 cup of brown rice per serving (page 73).

1 tablespoon extra-virgin olive oil
1 teaspoon dried Italian herb seasoning
2 cloves garlic, minced
Juice of 1 lemon
½ pound sirloin
1 red pepper
1 green pepper
1 onion
6 large mushrooms, thickly sliced
½ cup cherry tomatoes

Combine the olive oil, seasoning, garlic, and lemon juice in a small baking dish and blend with a fork. Cut the sirloin, peppers, and onion into chunks and add to the baking dish along with the sliced mushrooms. Toss and let sit at room temperature for 15 minutes. Preheat the broiler or heat a grill. Thread the meat and vegetables onto skewers, leaving spaces in between the individual foods so they will cook evenly. Cook for 4 minutes, turn and cook for another 4 to 6 minutes. Serve hot or cold.

DAY 24

Breakfast ❶ whole grains ❷ fruit ❸ protein

❶❸ 2 slices cinnamon-raisin bread with 2 tablespoons goat cheese

❷ 1 pear

1 cup freshly squeezed orange juice

Coffee or tea

(optional milk/sugar)

Lunch

Turkey Sandwich: 1 whole wheat pita spread with 4 tablespoons **Bean Dip** and stuffed with 3 ounces smoked turkey, 1 slice cheese (Comté or Swiss), 2 slices tomato, and ¼ cup lettuce.

1 cup grapes

Dinner

Vegetable Frittata

Whole grain roll

Mixed green salad with **Vinaigrette** (page 70)

Dessert: Melon

Buy a pedometer to find out how far you walk every day, and then increase your walking gradually for added health benefits.

RECIPES

Bean Dip   Makes 2 cups

Turn to this protein-rich mixture as a snack with raw veggies, or use in place of mayonnaise in sandwiches and wraps. It will keep for a week, tightly covered, in the refrigerator.

1 tablespoon extra-virgin olive oil
2 onions, sliced
1 (15-ounce) can black or pinto beans, garbanzos, or lentils
½ cup coarsely chopped walnuts

Heat the oil in a large skillet over medium heat. Add the onions and cook, stirring frequently, for 10 minutes, until they are very soft but not brown. Transfer the onions to a food processor along with the beans and walnuts. Blend for several minutes until smooth.

Vegetable Frittata   Serves 4

This is a perfect meal for lunch or a light supper. Serve with a green salad.

1 onion, diced
1 zucchini, diced
1 red or orange pepper, diced
2 tomatoes, diced
2 tablespoons extra-virgin olive oil
6 eggs

¼ cup grated Parmesan cheese
2 tablespoons diced fresh tarragon
   or 2 teaspoons dried
Salt and pepper
1 tablespoon extra-virgin olive oil

Heat the oven to 450°F. Arrange the vegetables on a lightly greased baking sheet, sprinkle with the olive oil, and bake for about 10 minutes, just until they are soft and the onion and zucchini are lightly browned on the edges. Remove from the oven and let cool.

Heat the broiler. Combine the eggs, cheese, tarragon, salt, and pepper in a large bowl, and whisk to blend. Heat the olive oil in a large, ovenproof skillet and add the egg and cheese mixture. Spoon the vegetables gently on top of the eggs, without mixing them in. Cook on the stove top over medium heat for a few minutes. When you can lift up an edge of the frittata and see that the bottom has browned, put skillet under broiler and cook for a few minutes, until the top is lightly browned. Watch carefully to prevent burning. Set the skillet on the stove top and let cool for a few minutes. Then slide the frittata onto a serving plate or cut into wedges and serve.

DAY 25

Breakfast ❶ whole grains ❷ fruit ❸ protein

❶ 2 slices whole wheat toast with 1 tablespoon apple butter

❷ 1 cup mixed fruit

❸ 6 ounces Greek yogurt

Coffee or tea

(optional milk/sugar)

Lunch

Lentil Salad

1 whole wheat pita

Or Leftovers: Use a slice of leftover cold **Vegetable Frittata** from Day 27 dinner as a filling for a sandwich made with hummus and whole-grain bread.

1 orange

Dinner

Scallops with Lemon and Spinach

Quinoa

Roasted sweet potatoes and onions

Dessert: Pears

Lentil Salad   Serves 4

Here's a meal that can also double as a light supper. Cook more lentils than you need for one meal and freeze them in individual portions so you'll always have some on hand.

1 cup lentils   ¼ cup chopped parsley (optional)
Juice of 1 lemon   1 can tuna, drained and flaked
4 cloves garlic, minced   2 cups salad greens
2 medium tomatoes, diced   Salt and pepper

Rinse the lentils and combine in a large saucepan with 1½ cups of water. Bring to a boil, reduce the heat to a simmer, cover, and cook for 20 minutes, or until the lentils are tender. Drain and let cool slightly. Combine the cooled lentils with the lemon juice, garlic, tomatoes, parsley, and tuna, and toss gently to mix. Serve on a bed of lettuce.

Scallops with Lemon and Spinach   Serves 4

Be sure to pat the scallops dry before you cook them, so they will brown evenly. Include 1 cup of cooked quinoa per serving.

1 pound scallops
1 tablespoon extra-virgin olive oil
2 cloves garlic, sliced into thin slivers
Juice of 1 lemon
½ pound fresh spinach, washed, stemmed,
    and cut into thin slivers
Salt and pepper

Place a clean towel on the counter, arrange the scallops in a single layer on it and gently pat them dry. Heat the olive oil in a large skillet. Sauté the garlic over medium heat for several minutes without browning. Add the scallops, and sear on all sides until browned, about 4 minutes total. Add the lemon juice and spinach, toss, and cook just until the spinach wilts. Season with salt and pepper.

DAY 26

Breakfast ① whole grains ② fruit ③ protein

①③ 2 whole grain English muffin halves with
1 tablespoon peanut butter

② 1 cup melon cubes

Coffee or tea

(optional milk/sugar)

Lunch

Shrimp and Barley Salad: 5 cooked shrimp, ½ bell pepper, 1 stalk
celery (chopped), 2 teaspoons capers, and ½ cup cooked barley
tossed with **Herb Vinaigrette** (page 70).

1 cup blueberries

Dinner

Zucchini-Chicken Couscous

Green salad with **Avocado Dressing** (page 70)

Dessert: Raspberries

Zucchini-Chicken Couscous   Serves 4

Shredded zucchini, which you can make in seconds in a food processor, cooks quickly and adds moisture and flavor to leftover grains.

1 tablespoon extra-virgin olive oil
1 onion, diced
2 teaspoons dried oregano
1 medium zucchini, shredded or grated
2 cups cooked whole wheat couscous
2 cups chopped, cooked chicken
2 tablespoons Parmesan cheese

Heat the olive oil in a skillet, add the onion, and sauté for 5 minutes over medium heat, or until the onion is soft but not brown. Stir in the oregano and cook for 1 minute longer to release its fragrance. Add the zucchini, stir, and cook for four minutes, or until the zucchini softens and releases moisture. Add the couscous and chicken, toss with a fork to blend well, and cook for three minutes. Add the cheese and cook for two minutes longer, just until the mixture is heated through.

Roast vegetables to bring out their sweet flavors. Cut up a selection of fresh vegetables, toss them with olive oil, scatter on a baking sheet or two, and roast at about 425°F. Asparagus spears, peppers, mushrooms, onions, and zucchini need about 10 to 15 minutes; sweet potatoes, winter squash, potatoes, carrots, turnips, and whole Brussels sprouts can take 20 to 25 minutes. Experiment. The goal is to have vegetables that are soft, sweet, and lightly browned around the edges. Eat some hot. Store leftovers in the refrigerator to microwave for other dinners or enjoy cold in salads and sandwiches.

DAY 27

Breakfast ❶ whole grains ❷ fruit ❸ protein

❶ 1 whole wheat pita

❷ 1 cup raspberries

❸ 1 large egg, scrambled with ½ chopped bell pepper, 1 small chopped onion, and 1 ounce Kasseri cheese.

Coffee or tea

(optional milk/sugar)

Lunch

Weekday Salad: ½ cup diced, cooked chicken with 3 artichoke hearts, 6 cherry tomatoes, ¼ avocado, 2 tablespoons goat cheese, ½ cup mixed greens, tossed with **Lemon Vinaigrette** (page 70).

Or Leftovers: Reheat leftover **Zucchini-Chicken Couscous** from Day 26 dinner.

Whole wheat pita

1 cup sliced plums

Dinner

Pasta with Peas

Mixed green salad with **Avocado Dressing** (page 70)

Dessert: Chocolate sorbet

Pasta with Peas   Serves 4

Make this simple weeknight supper in about 15 minutes. To vary the flavor, add some shredded carrots along with or in addition to the peas.

2 eggs, beaten
½ cup grated Parmesan cheese
1 cup frozen peas
12 ounces whole wheat linguini
1 tablespoon extra-virgin olive oil
1 large onion, thinly sliced
Salt and pepper

Bring a large pot of water to a boil. Combine the eggs and cheese in a small bowl, beat, and set aside. Put the peas in a strainer, rinse under hot water, and set aside. Break the linguini in half and cook according to the package directions. While the pasta is cooking, heat the olive oil in a large skillet. Add the onion and sauté for several minutes, until it softens. Add the peas to the skillet and cook for about 1 minute. Drain the pasta and add to the skillet. Toss gently to mix. Create a well in the center, add the eggs and cheese, and cook until they are starting to firm up. Toss with the pasta and cook for another 2 minutes. Season with salt and pepper and serve hot.

Frozen Vegetables
Keep several bags of frozen veggies on hand at all times at home (add to any recipe!) and at work (a bowl of microwaved peas and corn is an easy, fiber-filled snack).

DAY 28

Breakfast ❶ whole grains ❷ fruit ❸ protein

❶ 2 slices whole wheat toast

❷ 1 cup strawberries

❸ 6 ounces Greek yogurt

   ½ medium avocado

   Coffee or tea

   (optional milk/sugar)

Lunch

Mediterranean Pita Pizza

Or Leftovers: Reheat leftover **Pasta with Peas**
   from Day 27 dinner.

1 cup fruit salad

2 oatmeal raisin cookies

Dinner

Tuna with White Beans, Celery, and Peppers

Brown rice

Sliced tomatoes and cucumbers with **Vinaigrette** (page 70)

Dessert: Blackberry sorbet

Mediterranean Pita Pizza   Serves 4

Be creative in choosing vegetable toppings: red, orange, or yellow peppers, thinly sliced onions or carrots, sliced spinach. If you use fresh chopped spinach, add it before you add the cheese.

4 small whole-grain pitas
1 cup tomato sauce
½ cup (4 ounces) shredded mozzarella cheese
4 cups sliced mixed vegetables
4 teaspoons extra-virgin olive oil

Heat the oven to 350°F. Arrange the pita rounds on a baking sheet. (Use two sheets if necessary.) Using the back of a spoon, spread about ¼ cup of tomato sauce evenly on top of each pita. Top each pizza with some grated cheese. Arrange your choice of vegetables on the top, then drizzle with olive oil. Bake for 15 to 20 minutes, or until the cheese is lightly browned.

Tuna with White Beans, Celery, and Peppers   Serves 4

This is a perfect meal for a weekday dinner when you need to rely on what's in the pantry. And it tastes delicious cold, so bring leftovers to work. Include 1 cup of cooked brown rice per serving (page 73).

1 tablespoon extra-virgin olive oil
1 onion, sliced
2 stalks celery, sliced
1 red or yellow bell pepper, seeded and sliced
1 (15-ounce) can cannellini beans, drained and rinsed
1 can tuna, drained
½ cup thinly sliced fresh basil or baby spinach leaves
Salt and pepper

Heat the olive oil in a large skillet over medium heat. Add the onion, celery, and pepper and sauté for several minutes. Stir in the beans and cook for 2 minutes longer. Add the tuna and break it up slightly with a spatula. Add the basil and cook just until it wilts. Season with salt and pepper. Serve hot or at room temperature.

Salad Dressing

Dressings add a lot of flavor to green, grain, and pasta salads. They can also add a lot of calories and fat, so it pays to measure what you're using. Get into the habit of making your own simple salad dressings to bring clean, sharp flavor to all kinds of salads. Keep a container of dressing on hand for drizzling a small amount (1 tablespoon per person or less) on salads or cooked vegetables.

Vinaigrette
Makes ¾ cup

¼ cup cider or wine vinegar
½ cup extra-virgin olive oil
¼ teaspoon salt

Combine all ingredients in a jar with a tight fitting lid and shake until well blended.

Variations:

Balsamic Vinaigrette:
Use balsamic vinegar.

Herb Vinaigrette:
Add 1 tablespoon fresh chopped thyme, tarragon, or rosemary to the dressing.

Lemon Vinaigrette:
Add the juice of 1–2 lemons.

Honey-Mustard Vinaigrette:
Add 1–2 minced garlic cloves, 1 teaspoon Dijon mustard, and 1 teaspoon honey.

Avocado Dressing
Makes about 1 cup

¼ cup fresh lemon or lime juice
1 small avocado
1 clove garlic, minced
½ cup extra-virgin olive oil
Salt and pepper

Combine the juice, avocado, and garlic in a food processor or blender and puree. With the machine running, slowly add the oil. Season to taste with salt and pepper.

Yogurt-Herb Dressing
Makes about 1 cup

¾ cup plain Greek yogurt
1 clove garlic, minced
1 tablespoon Dijon mustard
1 tablespoon fresh tarragon or
  1 teaspoon dried
⅓ cup chopped fresh parsley
Salt and pepper

Combine yogurt, garlic, mustard, and herbs in a food processor or blender and puree. Season to taste with salt and pepper.

TIPS FOR HEALTHIER EATING

Here are some easy ways to make gradual but important changes in the way you eat.

- **Experiment with making different types of salads.** You don't need to get stuck in the lettuce-tomato-dressing rut. Fruits, beans, fish, cheeses, olives, and a variety of greens offer endless combinations.

- **Pick a different raw veggie each week for afternoon snacking.** Enjoy carrot sticks, bell pepper strips, or cucumber slices with 1 tablespoon of hummus or nut butter.

  - **Eat fruit as an afternoon snack, too.** Fruit provides vitamins and nutrients, and satisfies the sweet tooth without the dangers of a sugar crash afterwards.

  - **On weekends, make a pot of soup for the week ahead.** Freeze into single or double serving portions, and you can grab one for a quick lunch fix or for dinner.

- **Keep homemade trail mix in an airtight container in the kitchen.** Every week top it off, changing up the mix of nuts and dried fruits. No time for breakfast? Grab a handful. A small amount is very filling.

- **Use canned, rinsed beans (black, pinto, chickpeas, white).** Add to pasta dishes, salsas, and salads as for an inexpensive fiber and protein boost.

- **Dilute fruit juice.** With half sparkling water the calories are cut in half. Or, instead of drinking juice, have a piece of fruit and a glass of water.

- **Measure snack foods (popcorn, chips).** Instead of eating directly out of the bag, pour into a bowl, especially when relaxing in the evening. Limit your snack to about 1 cup.

- **Drink lots of water.** You've heard it a million times, but once more won't hurt. Oftentimes when we think we are hungry, we are actually slightly dehydrated.

- **At a restaurant, eat half (or less) of the food that's served.** Take the rest home for lunch or dinner the next day. Or, share an appetizer, entree, and dessert with your dining companion. Savor all the elements of a quality meal while keeping calories in check and eating smaller portions.

A Guide to Whole Grains

What's a Whole Grain?

Whole grains have three edible parts: the outer bran layers, rich in fiber and B vitamins; the germ, full of antioxidants; and the starchy endosperm.

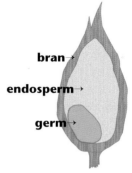

bran→

endosperm→

germ→

If the bran and the germ (the healthiest parts) are removed, the grain is said to be refined. Refined grains are missing about two-thirds of many essential nutrients. Some grains are then enriched – but this returns only about five of the many missing nutrients.

Your best bet for good health? Look for whole grains. Even if they've been ground into flour, rolled into flakes, or mixed into pasta or bread, they're whole grains if all of the three original parts are still present in their original proportions.

Finding Whole Grains

Whole grains are a key part of the traditional Mediterranean Diet. Barley, corn (including cornmeal and popcorn), oats (including oatmeal), quinoa, rice (both brown and colored), wheat (including farro and bulgur) and wild rice are among the whole grains sold in most supermarkets today.

Look for products that display the Whole Grain Stamp (above), which tells you how much whole grain is in a serving. To learn more about whole grains, visit **wholegrainscouncil.org**.

Cooking Traditional Mediterranean Grains

A rich golden corn polenta. Whole wheat couscous. Bulgur mixed with cucumbers, tomatoes, mint and parsley to make tabbouleh. A savory risotto. Traditional Mediterranean dishes offer a wide variety of options for enjoying more whole grains.

Cooking grains is easy. Just bring some water or broth to a boil (usually about 2 cups for each cup of grain), add your grain, then simmer gently until all the water is absorbed. Cooking time varies from none—for fine bulgur or for couscous, which simply absorb the boiled water in 15 to 20 minutes—to as much as an hour for grains like barley. Check package for exact instructions.

Barley: Look for hulled or hull-less barley; pearled barley is not a whole grain. Add barley to vegetable soups and stews, or combine with cucumbers, onions and feta for a grain salad. Many people also make barley "risotto."

Bulgur: Bulgur can be finely ground or coarse. Coarse bulgur may need to be simmered for 5 minutes and then left covered for 20 minutes or so, to absorb its liquid. Fine bulgur can be simply added to boiling water or broth, then left covered for 20 minutes or more while you cook the rest of your meal. Use it to make **Tabbouleh** (page 47); mix with walnuts and lemon juice to stuff peppers; or simply enjoy it as a side dish instead of rice.

Brown Rice: Use long grain for pilafs, and short grain for creamy risottos. Look for red rice, black rice and other colors that are also whole grain!

Couscous: Couscous is not a grain (there are no couscous plants!) but instead, is a small pasta-like granule made from either refined wheat or whole wheat. Look for the whole wheat kind, and simply add boiling water, then wait 15 to 20 minutes. Serve with stews or North African curries.

Farro: Farro is a kind of wheat traditional to Italy. Look for whole farro (not pearled, or "semi-perlato"). Use it in salads, stews, or side dishes.

Time-Saving Tips

While it's not too hard to get water going for a pot of quicker-cooking whole grains, it's even easier on a busy night to simply reheat what's waiting for you, cooked, in the refrigerator or freezer. Try cooking grains on the weekend when you're doing something else in the kitchen. Store leftovers in the refrigerator up to five days, or freeze portions in zip-lock bags to reheat in the microwave or toss by the handful into stews and soups.

SNACKS AT A GLANCE

Reach for one of these snacks, or a combination of several, if you want to expand your daily calorie intake. Add one of these foods to the daily menus as an afternoon pick-me-up, and/or as a dessert for lunch or dinner.

Note: The totals below reflect estimates. Check the specific nutrition labels on any products you purchase.

Snack	Serving Size	Calories	Fat (g)	Sat Fat (g)	Sodium (mg)	Carbs (g)	Fiber (g)	Protein (g)
Almonds	1 ounce (¼ cup)	160	14	1	0	5	3	6
Apple	1 medium	80	0	0	0	21	4	0
Baba ghanoush	1 tablespoon	20	1	0	25	2	1	1
Bean Dip	2 tablespoon	50	2.5	0	55	6	1	1
Biscotti	1 medium	100	5	1	50	11	2	6
Cantaloupe	1 cup	60	0	0	15	13	1	1
Cheese (Brie)	1 ounce	95	8	5	120	0	0	6
Cheese (Feta)	1 ounce	75	6	4	310	1	0	4
Cottage Cheese	½ cup	80	1	1	460	3	0	14
Carrots (baby)	6	25	1	0	50	6	0	0
Cashews (raw)	1 ounce (1/4 cup)	160	12	2	90	9	1	5
Cherries	1 cup	90	0	0	5	19	3	1
Chocolate (dark)	1 ounce	140	10	4	30	15	1	2
Cookies (oatmeal raisin)	2	210	7	2	200	20	2	3
Crackers (whole grain)	3	60	2	1	90	9	2	2
Dates	4	90	0	0	0	25	3	1
Figs (fresh)	2	70	0	0	0	19	3	1
Gelato (Vanilla)	½ cup	140	9	5	40	10	0	3
Grapes	1 cup	100	0	0	0	25	1	1

Snack	Serving Size	Calories	Fat (g)	Sat Fat (g)	Sodium (mg)	Carbs (g)	Fiber (g)	Protein (g)
Hummus (average)	1 tablespoon	25	1g	0	55	2	1	1
Latte (with 1% milk)	1 cup	110	2	2	105	12	0	8
Mango	1 cup	110	0	0	0	28	3	1
Olives (Kalamata)	6	40	3	0	220	3	1	0
Orange	1 medium	60	0	0	0	14	3	1
Peanuts (roasted, unsalted)	1 ounce (1/4 cup)	160	14	3	0	6	3	9
Peanut Butter (smooth, unsalted)	1 tablespoon	90	8	1	60	3	1	4
Pita Bread	1 small	70	1	0	150	15	2	3
Pistachios	1 ounce (1/4 cup)	150	12	2	0	8	3	6
Popcorn (unbuttered)	2 cups	60	0	0	0	12	2	2
Sorbet (raspberry)	½ cup	100	0	0	0	15	1	0
Sunflower Seeds (hulled, roasted, without salt)	1 ounce (1/4 cup)	160	14	2	0	7	3	6
Trail Mix (average)	¼ cup	170	11	2	85	17	2	6
Yogurt, Greek (2%)	6 ounces	130	3.5	2	70	7	0	17
Walnuts	1 ounce (1/4 cup)	190	18	2	0	4	2	4

RECIPE INDEX & NUTRITIONALS

Page	Recipe	Calories	Fat (g)	Sat Fat (g)	Sodium (mg)	Carbs (g)	Fiber (g)	Protein (g)
	Fish and Seafood							
45	Herb-Baked Fish	210	8	2	200	0	0	33
31	Mussels Provencal	140	2	0.5	170	9	1	11
57	Pasta Shells with Clam Sauce	490	12	1	75	80	11	30
39	Salmon Kebabs	300	16	2	125	7	2	30
63	Scallops with Lemon and Spinach	150	5	1	230	6	1	21
27	Six-Minute Shrimp	200	9	1	170	5	1	24
15	Spicy Salmon	270	12	2	330	2	1	17
51	Ten-Minute Seafood Stew	200	6	1	400	12	1	24
69	Tuna with White Beans, Celery, and Peppers	240	5	1	420	28	2	20
58	Tuna Wrap	560	27	2.5	730	52	12	33
	Poultry							
53	Chicken Kebabs with Yogurt Sauce	160	1.5	0	95	4	0	32
17	Chicken with White Beans	280	7	1.5	370	23	6	33
35	Honey-Mustard Chicken and Vegetables	320	11	2	125	28	4	30
55	Mediterranean Chicken Wrap	370	15	1.5	490	31	6	29
47	Turkey Couscous	500	13	2.5	510	60	8	38
65	Zucchini-Chicken Couscous	250	7	2	45	22	2	24
	Meat							
33	Oven-Roasted Pork Tenderloin	270	13	3	150	1	3	34
25	Sirloin Ribbons	270	13	4	75	1	0	35
59	Vegetable-Beef Kebabs	190	8	2.5	40	11	3	20

RECIPE INDEX & NUTRITIONALS

Page	Recipe	Calories	Fat (g)	Sat Fat (g)	Sodium (mg)	Carbs (g)	Fiber (g)	Protein (g)
	Meatless							
29	Cauliflower with Chickpeas	260	9	1	590	40	10	9
49	Cherry Tomato and Olive Pizza	240	6	2.5	690	37	6	11
15	Fresh Vegetable Wrap	440	17	1	520	65	10	11
69	Mediterranean Pita Pizza	310	10	4	230	40	8	16
45	Mediterranean Scramble	240	17	4	370	9	3	14
39	Mushroom Pita	330	14	4	310	48	5	9
37	North African Vegetable Curry	170	8	4	270	23	5	3
49	Open-Face Roasted Vegetable Sandwich	260	10	1.5	460	35	7	9
55	Pasta with Avocado Sauce	410	17	2	7	63	12	10
41	Pasta with Spinach and Beans	530	13	3	520	87	10	23
21	Pasta with Fresh Tomatoes	240	4.5	.5	0	50	6	6
67	Pasta with Peas	480	11	4	310	72	10	21
23	Roasted Vegetable Wraps	380	16	2.5	430	53	9	8
43	Spinach-Mushroom Strata	340	17	7	430	30	4	18
53	Tomato-Goat Cheese Wrap	290	20	6	550	23	10	16
61	Vegetable Frittata	270	20	5	230	9	2	13
27	Veggie Omelet	150	12	2.5	75	4	2	7
	Soups							
19	Lentil Soup	210	10	3	270	21	5	9
31	Minestrone	260	6	1	300	41	9	10
35	Spicy Carrot-Ginger Soup	90	3	1	480	16	4	2

RECIPE INDEX & NUTRITIONALS

Page	Recipe	Calories	Fat (g)	Sat Fat (g)	Sodium (mg)	Carbs (g)	Fiber (g)	Protein (g)
	Sides & Salads							
21	Baby Spinach with Feta and Almonds	140	11	3	240	5	2	6
33	Citrus Salad	420	34	3	85	30	8	8
17	Fattoush	250	13	4	400	31	7	9
25	French Potato Salad	230	5	1	75	44	5	5
29	Greek Salad	130	15	2	250	16	3	4
63	Lentil Salad	130	1	0	150	16	5	16
23	Mediterranean Salad	330	15	3	260	31	9	21
24	Meze Plate	220	8	3	410	27	4	10
43	Shrimp Salad	300	16	3	360	15	4	23
51	Spinach-Orzo Salad	470	16	3	490	72	17	14
47	Tabbouleh	140	1	0	55	30	10	6
37	Turkey-Apple Spinach Salad	380	16	6	290	33	7	26
67	Weekday Salad	290	16	5	160	9	4	27
	Dips, Dressings, and Spreads							
61	Bean Dip	50	2	.5	55	6	1	1
19	Guacamole	30	3	.5	60	2	1	0
70	Herb Vinaigrette	80	9	1	50	1	0	0
70	Honey-Mustard Vinaigrette	80	9	1	60	1	0	0
70	Lemon Vinaigrette	80	9	1	50	1	0	0

INDEX

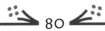